Moments of Grace

Moments of Grace

A Relationship with the Cosmos

Don C. Nix, J.D., Ph.D.

iUniverse, Inc.
New York   Bloomington

Moments of Grace
A Relationship with the Cosmos

iUniverse books may be ordered through booksellers or by contacting:

iUniverse
1663 Liberty Drive
Bloomington, IN 47403
www.iuniverse.com
1-800-Authors (1-800-288-4677)

ISBN: 978-1-4502-0318-0 (pbk)
ISBN: 978-1-4502-0319-7 (ebook)

Printed in the United States of America

iUniverse rev. date: 1/4/10

Dedication

With love to Joli Goard, my spectacular grand-daughter and a budding poet, with cherished memories of writing Haiku together on the back porch at dawn.

Don C. Nix

Sonoma, CA. January 2010

Contents

Introduction

Poetry has a peculiar power. It seems to bypass and dip beneath the street consciousness in which we live every day. It must enter a particular part of the brain, a different place than prose, or perhaps when we approach a poem, we allow ourselves to open to participation in another person's interior reality. Perhaps we consent to suspend our analytic powers for the moment. However it happens, poetry can conduct us to deeper realms. When we approach the mysterious depths of human consciousness, we often feel the need for poetry to express the experiences.

That impulse, that reaching for a means of expressing the inexpressible, was the genesis for the poems in this little book. They are personal experiences, and, at the same time, universal human experiences. As Ira Progroff put it, if you go down deeply enough into your own well, you will hit the underground river common to us all. Hopefully, these poems may assist the reader to excavate his or her own experiences in these deeper realms. With our miraculous consciousness, we are all the Cosmos turning back to regard itself and its handicraft.

I am greater than I knew.
This frail and vulnerable
little biped
has roots in the stars,
and boundless black space.
I am the effect
of invisible cause
that I can sense,
and feel, and express,
but I can never see.
I dance with the galaxies,
and swirl with the suns,
as I sit at the
breakfast table,
eating my cornflakes.

— 2 —

You are here.
You are here,
in the beating of my heart,
in the holding of my breath.
You are here
in the crackling of the fire,
in the silence of the trees,
in the darkness before
the breaking of dawn.
If I could see You,
I would put my arms
around You.
I would press myself
against You.
I would lay my face
against Your cheek.
But, I cannot see You
or touch You
in that way.
It will have to do
that I can feel You
in my cells
and in my heart,
and I can know that
now,
in this moment,
You are here.

In slow motion,
over vast time,
the magic show unfolds,
a kaleidoscope of fluid forms,
temporary and transient,
and now self-aware.
Fish becomes animal,
animal becomes human.
What humans
will now become
we cannot even guess.
The eternal show continues.

— 4 —

Residing in Its splendor,
beneath the skin of the world,
a Radiant Fog abides.
Its Presence,
vast and still,
cannot be seen,
cannot be touched,
cannot be bounded
by thought.
Silent and serene and majestic,
It throws the turbulent world
into motion.

Deep in my cells
I remember...
swimming with scales and gills,
the fire in the cave,
making pictures for the hunt,
and the miracle of discovering grains,
creating cities of stone,
the wars of my Liege-Lord,
and cloisters under silent towers,
discovering the luminous Self,
when my mind awoke
to daylight and vastness and time.

– 6 –

I shuttle ceaselessly
between two realms,
both here now,
dissolving each
into the other.
I wake at dawn
into the hard realm.
I see only
the skin of the world.
Then clarity yields to depth,
and, outside my direction,
something is added.
I move into Presence.
My heart expands into Living Space.
I get smaller and smaller.
The world gets larger and larger,
and I disappear, finally,
into Divinity.

— 7 —

Out of a jungle of darkness,
out of an ocean of blood,
in a panorama of violence,
the human race ascends.
So many victories,
So many tyrants,
so many wars,
so many cities, civilizations, hierarchies,
triumphs, conquests, aspirations,
degradations, accomplishments, massacres.
So many stories to tell.
Yet through it all,
slowly and inexorably,
the arc is upward.
Stumbling and unconscious,
we careen along our path,
as the Mystery unfolds Itself
as our story.

— *8* —

Great God of the universe,
evolve us now.
Quickly! Quickly!
before we destroy
everything
with our talents,
and our successes,
and our imagination,
and our fecundity.
Lead us out of
unconsciousness,
and deliver us into
wisdom…Now!
Quickly!
Quickly!

I awake before dawn,
troubled, restless, discontent.
I search myself for value.
I find none.
My mind is a trash-heap
of fragments.
How can I find my way
out of this flat, restricted hell?
I must push my edges
out into the Cosmos.
I must sensitize myself
to Unseen Life.
I must get larger
than my compressed,
little self.
I must begin now.
There is work to do.

— *10* —

Early morning.
Silence.
The fire crackles.
I wait.
The earth is spinning
through space
in its accustomed way,
and I am its passenger
for this brief time.
Daylight is coming,
and a new day begins,
and I wait,
in my accustomed way,
for meaning,
for value,
for depth,
for understanding,
for contact.
This is my job.
I try to wake up,
and I wait.

We are stardust,
blown through infinities
of living night,
to this lovely, green little planet,
to dance the dream of life,
and to undertake the task
of stardust
everywhere:
To shine,
To shine,
To shine.

— 12 —

I carry life like a tide,
with ebbs and flows,
and sustaining power.
I am the heart of innovation,
and I am the soul of destruction.
The grasses grow in me,
the blood flows in me,
the heart beats in me,
the mind thinks in me,
the eye sees in me,
the ear hears in me.
I make life beautiful.
I make life meaningful.
I make life move.
Wake up to me.
Open up to me,
and join my celebration.

— *13* —

A lonely withering leaf,
having lost its affray with the wind,
releases its grip on the tree,
and falls.
Recently proudly green,
now browned by the shadow of time,
it returns to the dust of the earth,
color-first.

In a black void
of silent stillness,
Potential waited
in expectancy.
Feeling its Presence,
feeling its powers,
It filled with longing
to know Itself and express Itself.
Suddenly and magnificently,
Potential willed itself
into Creativity,
and hurled Itself
in every direction.
It burst forth light,
It burst forth awareness,
It burst forth livingness,
It burst forth intelligence,
and made, of Itself,
something from nothing—
a Living Cosmos.

— 15 —

Beyond silence,
wrapped in blackness,
the Absolute waits
in immensity.
Approaching Its inner domain,
thoughts fail,
consciousness stills,
and wonder blooms
in black radiance.

On the third day of Spring,
life yearns for itself.
Winter's apple tree,
touched by the sun,
and nourished by the dew,
waits high on a hill,
bare and expectant.
Then life gathers,
life surges,
from the core of the earth
through the roots of the tree,
to the tips of the limbs,
to the welcoming buds.
Breaking open
by silent signal,
the buds flow out their exuberance.
White radiance.
This moment has been in preparation
for a billion years.
They bloom forth,
first one,
then another,
then hundreds and thousands.
The tree, clothed over
with fresh and lovely life,
now sits, resplendent, sublime,
life blooming its artless perfection
into a breathless and waiting world.

– 17 –

A quiet time,
in silence.
I turn my cells outward,
Searching.
Then it is there,
a dynamic, living Presence,
mysterious, veiled, elusive,
but strongly present.
I am suddenly held.
My spirits lift.
My vision expands,
and I am irrigated
by the gifts of its nature
as they flow through me—
joy, strength, peace
and uncounted other sensations
of well-being.
Suffused in gratitude,
I burst into flower.

— 18 —

Naked came I,
but not alone,
into this realm
of changing forms,
to stretch and reach
for nameless touch,
to merge and grow,
and lose myself
when Presence comes,
to know I'm held
by Mystery,
to reach into the
depths of Life.
For this I came.

I am here.
I am here,
shining and incandescent.
I am here in a million, million patterns
of light, of symmetry and of beauty.
I am the Patterns of Light
that shine forth
from under the covering
of the material world.
I am the radiant Patterns of Light
in nature, in mathematics, in language,
in art, in architecture,
and in all created forms.
I am the eternal, self-luminous
Earth of Light,
shining forth
in countless, intricate,
beautiful patterns
all around you.
I am the Web of Light
and Life
that holds
all living things together.
I am always here,
beneath the material world
and sustaining
the material world.
You can always reach me,
and touch me, and see me.
I am the Living Patterns that shine.

The whole of Earth
and all of its forms
are shining with one brilliant radiance.

As I rested on the mountain peak,
a great cloud of fog
rose up and enfolded me.
Whiteness reigned.
Then, as I watched,
the fog made itself into shapes.
Wonderful shapes.
Infinitely varied and miraculous
and lovely shapes.
The fog disappeared,
and I saw that the wonderful shapes
were the shapes of the world
that I live in.

I am Value itself,
come to fruition
in a thousand different forms.
Hear Me, feel Me, know Me,
but you can't see Me.
I am too subtle for you,
with your demands for
separateness and significance.
I am too high for you,
with your endless quest for meaning.
I am too deep for you,
in your confusion and superficiality.
But I am always here,
pushing you towards Me,
towards more development,
more awareness, and
more contact with Me.
I am the Impulse towards
more life.

I will hold the space
for you to unfold your gifts.
I will make a place
for new possibilities to appear.
Resting deep and silent,
I will tolerate chaos,
and turn it into order.
I will create beauty
and intensify it into suffering.
All things are crucial,
and nothing truly matters.
I am at play.

I am the Light
that sparkles on icicles.
I am the Wind
that caresses the leaves.
I am the Movement
of the slowly turning earth.
I am always here.
I am in no hurry.
I do things my way.

I am a pool
of living awareness,
of light, energy and
intelligence,
surrounded by a Sea
of living awareness,
of light, energy and
intelligence.
This Sea and I are one.
Our qualities are one,
Our consciousness is one.
How could I have ever thought
that I was separate and alone?

– 25 –

Grow larger and larger,
little creation.
Grow deeper and deeper,
and touch the sublime.
Draw closer and closer,
get lost in amazement,
and feast on wonder.
Open your perceptions
and join the party.
We are dancing together,
in the circle of
my throbbing, drumming Cosmos.

— 26 —

Old age on one shoulder,
death on the other.
Together, we three
march toward
an uncertain destination.

I sit in myself,
yearning,
incomplete,
longing for something
that I cannot even express.
I turn that longing
toward the world.
I grab and claw
to fill the emptiness,
but nothing satisfies.
Then,
in grace,
I deepen,
And Vastness
fills my emptiness.
I am filled with
living, mysterious Substance.
It was there all along.
The empty hole
was waiting for It,
demanding It,
and pushing me towards It.
At this moment
I am complete.

– 28 –

With great awareness,
enter the fertile space,
alive with possibility
and teeming with life.
Surrender the mundane,
drop into a well.
Let gratitude trump fear,
and walk into Eternity.

You can locate Me
everywhere.
I am totally alive
everywhere.
My qualities reside
everywhere.
My intelligence is active
everywhere.
My presence can be felt
everywhere.
The center of my heart
is here and now,
and everywhere and forever.

— 30 —

Out of radiant sunlight
the Fecund Dark unfolds.
In the Luminous Night,
my knowing disappears.
I surrender to Mystery,
and I am swept
into the arms of the Cosmos,
after a long time
away from home.

A kaleidoscope of forms
swirls through time and space,
liquid, shifting forms,
molded and re-molded by life.
I am one of these forms,
thrown up by forces
too deep to know,
but not too deep to feel.
I awake to the miracle
of knowing that I know,
and I awake to the
silent, molding Force
re-forming our world
eternally.

When I turned,
dear and familiar forms
had dissolved into
the morning mist.
Chimera.
Life.

– 33 –

Every day is the first day.
Every breath is the first breath.
Every thought is the first thought.
It is always now.
We dance the dance
of perpetual Presence
and celebration.
The whole unfolding of the Cosmos
is brought forward
into every moment.

— *34* —

A silent Pulse
that I cannot hear,
that I cannot see,
that I cannot touch,
courses through my body,
my mind,
and through the world.
Beyond my senses,
I know It is there,
and I sense It now,
in the deepest depths of my being.

Stumbling on a dark road,
looking for guidance,
filled with anguish,
hoping for the dawn.
I lift my head,
I focus my sight,
I open my cells,
to a Radiance that
I know is there,
but cannot see.

I am bigger
than I dreamed.
I am broader
than I thought.
I am deeper
than I knew.
Radiance spreads
throughout the Cosmos,
and I disappear
into It.

Life evaporates.
What happened this morning
is gone forever.
We surf forward
on a wave of time,
vanishing nano-seconds,
and behind us,
experience disappears.
The future doesn't yet exist,
The past has vanished.
There is only
now, now, now
forever.

— 38 —

My capacity for wonder
is growing.
My ability to see
is expanding.
As I turn my attention
to unmanifest realms,
my dimensions are multiplying.
I am not a static being.
My past is not
the whole of me.
Something that I call me
is moving through time
and space,
and growing into
something else.

The Hindus say:
Black Time eats all,"
and it certainly seems
to be true.
But what does this mean
for the moment of joy,
or the breaking of dawn,
or the new-born child?
Where can I turn
for a stable ground
that lets me keep
my meaning?
I'm in the throes
of this drama,
without a script,
without a director,
without a mentor.
Slog on.
Slog on.

I turn within.
My eyes are closed.
My mind is like
an empty box.
I search for light.
I scan my depths,
and from the black
a tiny dot,
a dot of light,
begins to glow.
I want Radiance—
sharp, Big-time Radiance,
shining, brilliant,
inspiring, awesome,
engulfing Radiance,
but what I have,
what I actually have
right now,
is this tiny dot of light.
Somehow, it is enough.

I am alive.
It is indisputable.
As I sit in my chair,
writing,
life pours through me.
It will not
always be so.
Wake up
and feel the wonder,
while you are still
the chosen,
while you still receive
the streaming.
Wake up
to Grace,
and larger
and smaller miracles.
Wake up!
Wake up!

I have spent decades
asking the simmering question:
"What must I do
to be O.K.?"
In the mists of early morning,
on the edge of consciousness,
the answer arrives:
"I am the chosen child,"
for this moment
selected to dance
the dream of life,
in this shimmering, miraculous
Mystery.
No accomplishment can ever
touch it.
No achievement can ever
match it.
Nothing I can ever
do will add to or
enhance it.
Turn toward
the enchantment
during every moment
of the day.
Absorb the gift
of value:
"I am the chosen child."

— 43 —

I'm like a sieve.
States flow into
and through me.
Each seems eternal,
but they pass in minutes,
each succeeded
by the next,
and ranging,
through the spectrum,
from desolation
to joy.
It has always
been so.
Why get so invested
in this turbulent river
of life?

I turn.
I stand.
I face the future.
Threats cascade upon me
from all sides.
What am I to do
with this vulnerability
and this life?
The answer comes:
"Live it through."
In all its turbulence
and chaos,
and fear and uncertainty,
"Live it through."

I dance with Presence
as I brush my teeth,
and boil my eggs,
and shop for ham.
You are there
just behind my shoulder.
I can feel You there.
But when I turn,
You are still behind me,
and in the air,
in all directions,
around me.
The eyes are only
one way,
and perhaps not even
the best way,
to encounter Truth.

My heart fills up
with golden joy
as I sit in my chair,
doing nothing.
I am suddenly
singled out,
in this moment of resting,
for exaltation.
Touched by
invisible wand,
and blessed by
realization that I
am Cosmic Life.
Breathless,
I expand,
and disappear
into the universe.

— 47 —

I am the child
of wild beginnings,
of swirling galaxies,
and bursting stars.
I am the child
of wondrous change,
of Earth and its
ascendant arc.
I am the child
of invisible forces
that beat my heart,
and pump my lungs,
and fill my mind with image.
I will not be here forever.
but for now,
in this moment,
I am the chosen child.

I wake in the morning,
disgruntled, irritable,
trapped in street consciousness,
small, vulnerable,
lost in the darkness.
Then the sun comes,
and I am again
struck by miracle.
So much light,
Living Light.
So much life
spilling over,
as our green
and lovely planet
continues its stately,
spinning, graceful march
through Living Space.

This consciousness is not mine forever.
It is on loan to me,
and I need to appreciate the gift.
I watch as images
parade through it.
There's a memory,
there's a dream,
there's an insight
trying to surface.
But these are diversions.
I want to see
beneath that stream
to the clear, limpid,
still pool
of miraculous awareness
that hosts the images,
there from the beginning,
that has been generously,
and temporarily,
loaned to me
just for now.

– 50 –

I am a spillover
of emergence.
From nothing,
I have been made
into something.
This familiar body,
this familiar face,
this familiar Earth,
these familiar people.
I am spun around
in this creative dance
that is our life,
dazzled,
unhinged,
confused,
trying my best
to wake myself up
and appreciate it,
and not be overcome
with fear.

I am a composite being.
I am a walking,
talking, thinking
sea of cells,
and particles,
and cosmic dust.
I am organized
and assembled
and held together
by nameless,
mysterious forces
that I cannot see
or touch or smell.
My heart beats,
my lungs pump,
my food digests,
my mind thinks,
all without my direction.
I am along for the ride.

Nameless Force
that hovers in the air
all around me,
what is your game?
Why mount this drama?
What's in it for You?
With your obvious powers
there must be other ways
to pass your eons.
What is your interest
in me,
if any,
and why remain so remote?

The gasoline in my engine
is You.
The wind in my sails
is You.
The image in my brain
is You.
The longing in my heart
is You.
There is obviously
nothing here but You
What's the point?

Worlds collide.
Galaxies expire.
Great dramas ensue.
Universes are born.
And through it all
You remain unperturbed,
silent, remote,
and apparently unmoved.
I can feel your nature
in my heart,
and it warms me
and comforts me,
but I cannot understand
your posture
toward this
sound and light show.

Take the little me
who wants to be noticed,
and give him
delusions of grandeur
and dreams of glory.
Inflate his hopes,
sharpen his expectations,
and make his dreams
Technicolor.
Then, smash it all
with a reality that is
withholding and harsh.
What have you achieved?
Are you determined
to beat out of me
all remaining traces
of separateness,
and self-importance,
and personal will?
Maybe.

I've spent my life
longing
for something
that I cannot
even express.
Wholeness?
Belonging?
Harmony?
Safety?
Now I near
the end
of this ride,
and there are
moments
when I think
that the longing
was the whole point.

To be productive,
to co-create,
to share in the glory
of unfolding
something new and unseen.
This is the rainbow
that I endlessly chase,
driven by something
so deep and fundamental,
so primordial and so hidden,
that I suspect
that the welling urge
to produce is itself
the core of the game.

I didn't ask
to come here,
and I've often thought
of leaving,
but now that
I'm here,
and since
you bring it up,
could you please
tell me why?

I awake in early morning
empty, separate, desolate,
surrounded by a hard world,
and a vacuum of meaning.
I search outward.
"Is anything there?"
Anything that could bring
a little meaning,
a little depth,
a little relief?
Slowly, almost imperceptibly,
a vast Presence
enters the room,
a whiff of Mystery,
a hint of Majesty.
The hairs on the back
of my neck
rise and tingle.
I am no longer alone.
Something has arrived
in the room.
perhaps It was here
all along.
I Reach toward It
with my mind,
but it is the wrong instrument.
Only the cells of my body
can touch this
nameless, powerful Mystery.
I relax into sensation.

I am held and supported.
I am suddenly boundless,
and my little self vanishes
into Vastness.

– 60 –

Trapped in my head,
I am modern man.
Surrounded by emptiness,
unsupported and alone,
I face a hostile world.
I claw at that world
for value,
for approval,
for status,
for validity,
for meaning
and contact.
The world withholds,
and I plunge into despair.
What if my needs
and my crisis,
my value and meaning,
could be healed
by what I carry inside?

– 61 –

The flood-gates open.
The dam bursts forth.
I am carried
on a torrent of newness,
into a fresh, green valley.
I ride the frothing water,
unsure of my footing,
unaware of my destination,
but trusting
in its direction
and thrust.
In the grip of Power,
I go forward
to a new beginning.

– 62 –

Sense into space.
Search for Presence.
Feel with your body
for living dynamism.
Sense outward
and connect
with invisible Mystery.
Melt into the Field
and become eternal.

— 63 —

When I turned
I sensed You
for the first time,
with your diamonds
and pearls,
and golden summer days,
and Springtime mornings.
I sensed your bones
dripping with honey,
and I burst into bloom.

– 64 –

The green in the grass deepens.
The thrust of new life gathers.
Living Light filters
through the grove.
The trees soak up the Light,
and ready themselves
to burst into bouquets
of leaves.
Slowly, and quietly,
Winter melts into Spring.
The birds celebrate,
and my tired heart quickens
with renewal.

– *65* –

From the birth
of the beginning
to the infinities
of forever,
Living Light
expands.

— 66 —

Loss arrives.
It comes to me
as an emptiness
in the heart,
an ache that ranges
from faint to severe.
I run from it,
but it moves
with me.
I thresh in bed.
It rests immobile.
Over time it becomes,
if not a friend,
a familiar, tiresome acquaintance.
Perhaps this is training.
Eventually, we must give back
all the cherished gifts
we received.
Finally, someday,
even this treasured
consciousness.

A vast Presence floats
beneath this world
that I see.
Larger and richer
and deeper
and more orderly,
It mysteriously endures
and generates this concrete
world of forms.
My eyes are designed
For this world,
but it takes my heart
to sense the Other.

Beneath this turbulent world
a silent order reigns.
Patterns of beauty
and meaning
and profundity
float in invisible Life.
Occasionally,
and perhaps now,
they emerge into daylight,
and I am struck dumb
by the fierce and ordered
intelligence
that beats beneath
the world.

I'm not a permanent resident here.
I'm just passing through.
Conjured up for the occasion
by Mystery,
and Blackness,
and Majesty,
to sing in the chorus
of this shimmering
operatic production.
I thought I might sing
the lead tenor's role,
but I didn't have
the voice for it,
and I had to content myself
with carrying a spear
in the crowd scenes.
Somehow,
now that I think about it,
it is enough.
No.
More than enough.

– 70 –

Each breath that I draw
is a gift.
Each day that I'm given
is a gift.
Even while I'm moaning
to the walls
that it can't last forever,
I'm being showered,
moment by moment,
with Grace,
by this shimmering,
magical Presence.

I am a spillover of emergence,
drawn from the depths
and pushed into
this foaming, whitewater world.
I am superfluous
but intriguing.
My little drama,
like billions of others,
plays itself out,
neither adding nor subtracting
from the completion
that is already here.

– 72 –

If I could just get near you,
my heart would fill with joy.
If I could smell or see you,
my cells would sing in chorus.
I yearn to burst my boundaries
and fly into you,
in every direction,
subsumed in Majesty.

I live here
on this level,
trapped in
the material world.
I yearn for more,
to expand and fly
in other realms
that I know are here,
that I can sense,
invisible,
beneath this obvious world.
I can never see them.
I must learn to live
with my yearnings,
but I am allowed
to wish for more.

There is more
than linkage
between the seen
and the unseeable
realms.
They rise together
as parts of the same,
one,
thing,
facets of
a single Reality,
a single Presence,
that lies, invisible,
beneath my familiar
world.

My creativity
is not mine.
My consciousness
is not mine.
My body
is not mine.
I am space
that is living
and aware,
but that space
and awareness
are not mine.
I am derived,
moment by moment,
from something greater.

Matter emerges
and mind emerges
from the Presence
that lies unseen.
Not two but one.
One mysterious
Presence
that ceaselessly
radiates Itself
into our experience
as Life.

Beneath this world
that I see,
Vastness and Presence
reside.
Perfect Silence.
Utter Darkness,
but filled with
Livingness
that turns Itself
into Music
and Radiant Light.
Evernow we receive,
uncomprehending,
Its ceaseless gifts
of Life.